Beauty for Ashes:
Memoir of a Traumatic Brain Injury Survivor

Written by:
Alexis Lee

Cadmus Publishing
www.cadmuspublishing.com

Copyright © 2021 Alexis Lee

Published by Cadmus Publishing
www.cadmuspublishing.com

ISBN: 978-1-63751-054-4

All rights reserved. Copyright under Berne Copyright Convention, Universal Copyright Convention, and Pan-American Copyright Convention. No part of this book may be reproduced, stored in a retrieval system, or transmitted in any form, or by any means, electronic, mechanical, photocopying, recording or otherwise, without prior permission of the author.

Acknowledgement

First and foremost, I want to thank God for blessing me with this opportunity to share my life-changing experience with you. With my whole heart I dedicate this memoir to all the brave ones who live moment to moment with the reality of a scar that no one else can see or comprehend, regardless of how much they love you. The ones who have to find unique ways to put life's puzzle back together again—even if it means some of the pieces will never be replaced, or even fit at all. The caregivers, friends and loved ones who lace up your bootstraps to support and empower the person they once knew, the person who has changed… the person you're re-learning and re-loving. Thank-you, and I love you.

The Center for Disease Control and Prevention defines a traumatic brain injury (TBI) as a disruption in the normal function of the brain that can be caused by a bump, blow, or jolt to the head, or penetrating head injury.

None of what I am about to share is a figment of my imagination; however, names have been changed to protect the privacy of the individuals mentioned.

Dedication

A Tribute to My Irreplaceable Grandma

It is so hard to find the right words to use to talk about the person who saved my life, raised me, taught me about Jesus and initiated a lifelong relationship with my Abba. She spoiled me, always shared words of wisdom with me, always wanted the best for me and instilled a great yearning in me to be the best that I can be.

I never wanted to imagine that this day would come and now it is here. As the old saying goes, you taught me a lot, Grandma, but you never taught me how to live without you. I will try to go on, and I must, because it is what you would have wanted for me. I will forever keep your grace hidden in my heart. It is your tenacity that I have inherited and now I know why you had to be such an integral part of my journey.

My Ms. Ine was my friend, my first friend. I will forever miss her infectious laughter and breathtaking jokes.

I will love you always Ms. Ine.

Contents

The End and the Beginning 1

Refund My Student Loan… Please 14

Friendship Bracelet 53

Ways to Help 63

Surreal 64

Talitha Cumi 89

The End and the Beginning

It is important to note from the very beginning that as part of the course of my diagnosis I cannot recall all the events in their entirety. Nonetheless, I am sharing what I can so you might grasp my experience in its raw state, by categorizing major areas of impact in my life as opposed to detailing it in chronological order. In addition, being mindful of readers with cognitive impairments from a traumatic brain injury, I have tried not to make this a lengthy read. If as an adult you have never had the experience of having to relearn how to write your name, have had your baby sister help you with grade three addition and subtraction, or have even struggled with the simple skill of remembering how to get home—be thankful.

Maybe you had immediate and exciting plans with your loved ones, or your life may have been luxurious and comfortable, before *all of this* happened. Are you a caregiver, or an ally of someone who now depends on you for support and other services? Our lived experiences are unique; however, the beauty is in a shared sense of *knowing how it feels*. We may be diverse in culture, socioeconomic status, gender, or even political views but nevertheless, we all need compassion, love and understanding—especially during trauma and tragedy. Whatever the position you find yourself in while reading this book, ask yourself: what does compassion look like? If you have been diagnosed with a Traumatic Brain Injury, or are supporting someone who has, how can you be present and positive? I know, I know—I'm on the other side of recovery and probably sound as perky as a pigtailed camp counsellor, but I've learned that these are essential to pushing ahead with recovery, friend. Why, you may ask? Because, quite simply, as meaningless and innocent as a sigh may seem when you've been asked to help someone for the thirtieth time in a day, or are telling yourself that there is nothing to look forward to now in life, the truth is that this would be as productive as trying to push a door open that says pull.

Friend, I am praying that what I have to share will give you a sense of belonging and hope, to push back against the loneliness and isolation that comes with this condition. I want to spark positivity in you, which will make you feel like you *can* do this and feel a sense of relief that someone knows what it is like to have your whole world pulled right out from under your feet. I want you to know that you are not alone in your feelings of frustration and, at times, confusion. In essence, I want to speak life to you, I want to speak life into your situation, which you might feel is either dead or dying.

I am not going to say that I totally understand your lived experience, because our experiences are as unique as the fingerprints on our pinkies; therefore, what may not be an inconvenience to me might be the complete opposite for you. Maybe not being able to cook your own meals looks like a good excuse to get away from the kitchen for you, but for me it may mean I can't control how much gravy is going on my potatoes. What I *will* say is this: you have an ally. You have someone who may not know your name, face or number, but I do know pain and I do know loss and despair. I have experienced the invisible injury that no one is able to see, but that is judged based on its manifestations or lack thereof.

I am about to share with you my lived experience with a Traumatic Brain Injury (truthfully, I don't even want to capitalize the darn thing, but oh well). The trauma of losing my life as I knew it, losing relationships, experiencing isolation, and being treated like an invalid by so-called medical professionals sent me into an abyss of depression that no one should ever endure. *But,* most importantly, you will see my relationship with Christ (my Abba) blossom, from knowing Him as a dreadful and terrible God… to my Deliverer and Friend.

My Journey

I am an honors graduate; I went to college and university and thoroughly enjoyed all of my studies. For twelve years I worked in the court system, and for thirteen at a women's shelter assisting survivors of abuse. I grew up with my paternal aunt and uncle, Sadie and Earl, their four daughters, Charmaine, Debbie, Jackee and Charlene, and my beloved grandmother Inez who was an old-school Christian from Jamaica. To say they were strict was an understatement; however, in retrospect I realize that I was privileged.

Our home was in a quiet neighborhood, nestled in a cul-de-sac with the typical untouchable plastic-covered living room furniture most West Indian homes were famous for. We were known for hosting huge Christmas parties, and other gatherings. I wanted for nothing—everyone spoiled me as the baby of the family, especially Grandma and Earl. My biological mother, Pauline, wasn't out of the picture; I would spend some weekends with her and my twin brother and sister, Paul and Paula, who lived in a different city until the early 90s. My mom's home was heavily laden with all the toys you could imagine; she maintained rules, but they were nothing like the laws of Sadie and Earl.

My mom, a two-time beauty pageant queen in Jamaica, was stern about education, tact and decorum. She took no issue with Paul, Paula and I playing and having fun, just as long as our homework was completed, but if she noticed too many hours invested in games and the neighborhood children, she would reel us in and tell us, "Go and find a book," in her Uptown Kingstonian accent. Back in those days there were door-to-door salespeople who would sell large black encyclopedias filled with pictures and information covering just about anything and everything concerning the world—my mom bought them, and our job was to read them. At night she would sit in the bed with us while we read a portion of whatever we'd selected in those overweight books whether we wanted to or not (we weren't even teenagers yet).

At my aunt and uncle's, the key was cleanliness and making yourself useful. There were five of us girls in the home and we were always taught to keep the house clean, how to wash by hand and how to cook. We dared not go to bed with the kitchen untidy, or *everyone* had to get out of bed and start cleaning—when I was too short to reach the sink my duty was to hold the dustpan while someone else swept. Manners, principles and discipline were pretty much stamped on our foreheads. In those days, when adults were having a conversation, you ran to the furthest room you could find; also, *may I, please* and *thank you* were sure to be in order. My grandma was like Heaven's hall monitor; every night she would boldly ask if I had said my prayers before I jumped into her bed, and as soon as she saw me awake in the morning it was the same thing, not to mention her routine check-in of "Yuh study yuh Sunday school lesson, Alexis?" (Translation: did you study your Sunday school lesson, Alexis?) At night she would listen to The Grace Thrillers, Joseph Niles, Glen Graham and other gospel singers while whispering the words of the scriptures she was reading in the Bible—that was my lullaby.

At thirteen years old I became a baptized born-again Christian (just weeks before my first day of high school) which meant no pants, no jewelry, no secular music, no makeup—and absolutely no boyfriends. My uniform consisted of long-sleeved shirts and kilts that stretched way past my knobby knees, along with knee-high socks to finish the job of covering me up. I wish you could picture me around four feet eleven inches and probably ninety pounds soaking wet with a head full of hair bundled up in a simple bun and a big scrunchie (I hope you're giggling because it wasn't fun for me). Dress down days at school were the worst, because I only had long jean skirts while all the other girls wore fashionable jeans and cool outfits; eventually, I just decided to wear my uniform and tell everyone I forgot we could wear regular clothes (yeah, I know, I lied). I went to Bible Study on Wednesdays, youth meetings on Fridays, Sunday Service in the morning and evenings—along with Convocations and the holiday church picnics. I did it all as far as a "good Christian girl" went, but didn't know about a *relationship* with Christ, I just knew I had to follow the rules and I was terrified to break them. My understanding was *don't sin, or God will kill you!*

Growing up in the faith, I never felt like I could ever measure up to the standard of *holiness* as it was taught to me—so ultimately, I did my own thing and thought maybe I wasn't good enough for God or the people around me. Mind you, I still believed in Jesus and tried my best, but never felt like my best was good enough, because no matter how hard I tried I was still being told "You're going to hell," and the first time I wore pants in my twenties officially put me in the outcast section. Well, what did I do? I put my all into my education and career because that's where I felt accomplished—maybe even validated. I climbed and climbed to the best of my ability.

As an adult my hard work paid off in terms of my career path. Fast forward and I was *right there*—right at the edge of the biggest career jump of my life (as I knew it). Not only that, but I had also started my small business as a personal stylist. I had clients, and was so excited for where it was going. Nothing felt better than putting a fab outfit together for someone, then seeing their faces light up with satisfaction when they got "joojed" up. Styling was different. It was a whole new world from the court scene I was used to—it was my joy and passion. Positive vibes all around! By the time the accident came I had travelled—a *lot*. I took vacation time seriously. To me, it meant "Let's get the heck outta Dodge!" My getaways were always planned way in advance, with color-coded tabs on plane tickets, hotel confirmation printouts, and that kind of thing. If you're a traveler, you know the excitement of counting down the days to embarking on your liberation from the chaos. My petit feet have been blessed to touch the land and sands of nineteen countries (I still have a couple on my wish list to cross off). For a milestone birthday, I pranced on over to Paris for my first pair of Christian Louboutin heels.

Another fave of mine: food! You could always find me chowing down on a juicy piece of steak at a swanky restaurant with friends, or reading a good legal suspense novel with a glass of Moscato. There's nothing like the smell of a new book, with pristine pages that would soon meet the fate of having their corners turn into puppy ears as makeshift bookmarks. I often looked forward to trips to my local bookstore—it was my nearby escape—getting lost in the aisles of poetry, history, and giddy drama. I loved my life; things were great, and I had a budding relationship with a fun-loving guy named Mark whom I had reconnected with after a number of years.

Welp, here it begins, the catalyst that catapulted me toward lacing up my bootstraps and starting my life all over again. It was a beautiful summer day in 2017, and I was at the courthouse ready to go out for lunch, when I was delayed by half an hour to help some ladies, with criminal charges filed against them, to navigate the legal system. While walking in the parking lot to get a juicy grilled pineapple and brie cheeseburger, I felt this strong urge to keep my cell phone in my purse and change the Ray Charles CD I had been playing in my car to the Christian radio station—definitely something I couldn't ignore, so I did it. I put the key in the ignition and off I went.

"Can you feel your legs?"

This was said by a paramedic holding my neck. I couldn't hear properly from the loud ringing in my ears and everything was jumbled up and blurry.

My car had ended up in the back of an SUV.

While in the hospital, I only had X-rays of my hands, got some bandages and was embarrassingly greeted by the police. They sent me home. No head scan. I can't tell you more because it's all a big blur. I worked an hour away from home and had to call a coworker to help me. I waited in a hallway by myself until someone showed up to take me to the car lot to collect my things. Mind you, at this time I had no clue what I should or shouldn't be doing because I'd never been in an accident before. An officer gave me a ticket with a court date saying I was driving carelessly since I was the one who'd rear ended the other driver. How you might ask? I don't know. All I knew was I needed to show up for court. My internal reaction was *Show up for court? What the heck?!* How was I to appear *in* court when I worked there? How would this play out in front of the same people that I worked with? I didn't even know what my defense would be! I was tired, all of me was tired, and apparently there was more to this day that I needed to tackle.

Driving in my coworker's car went as quickly, as the lines on the road passed with every spin of the tires. I just wanted to go home. I think she was trying to cheer me up by saying she knew someone who was in an accident and went to work the next day. She spoke as if it was no big deal while I was fighting back tears brought on by physical pain and the shock of still not processing what had just happened. When we got to the Collision Centre the attendant bulged his eyes out at me and said: "*You?* You came out of *this?*"

My car, which I had affectionately named Juan Pedro, looked like the middle of a s'more. It was a write-off, mangled and unidentifiable with the front windshield totally smashed (enter the beginning of loss of independence here). I really didn't want to take anything home with me; the thing looked like a crime scene and smelled like smoke—it was repulsive. Ironically, I ended up taking a first aid kit I had in the trunk for emergencies and my shoes from the wrangled car. My coworker dropped me off at a nearby mall with the certainty that I'd be back in court the following week. I felt sick to my stomach.

My brother Paul didn't hesitate to make the long-haul drive to pick me up from where I sat alone on a mall bench, bandaged and shaken—sitting alone again for the second time during this traumatic day. I don't remember the ride home, but I do remember saying, "Don't tell Mom." I didn't want her to worry; in fact, I didn't want anyone to worry because in my mind this would all settle over the weekend and I would be fine—since everyone made it seem there was no serious injury and it had *just* been an accident.

ALEXIS LEE

Refund My Student Loan… Please

I am going to tell you that "pain" is an expression that can only be understood by the one carrying that cross. I went to the doctor the following day to tell him I was in a car accident and felt like crap—to say the least. He took the big bandage off my forearm and said, "That's a second-degree burn!" My skin was white and sore, like something from a science lab; the ER doctor hadn't given me any burn medication to follow it up—just a white bandage. My doctor was so kind and gentle (I mention this because I can't share the same sentiment for the vast majority of other overpaid white coats I met for the next two and a half years). He registered me for six counselling sessions because I told him I was afraid to drive again, and other follow-up appointments with his office. I was sore, my body was in so much pain and I could hardly move. Brushing my teeth and showering were even lengthier than what the average woman would account for.

Maybe a day or two after that I was in my grandma's old room (she had passed two years prior, and my dad followed the year after—and my grandpa after that—yeah, I know, right?) and all of a sudden, I recall the room going black and I wanted to throw up. My sister-in-law, Natalee, rushed me to the hospital and it was one of the worst car rides ever. I remember crying because I was terrified and dizzy; the motion of her car didn't make it any easier for me. "You've got a little bit of a concussion," is what the doctor said based on my symptoms; although she was kind and gentle, again I left with no head scans, just a rushed smile and an information sheet telling me to stay away from the phone and TV screens for 24 hours, along with hourly check-ins from family members whenever I fell asleep.

Please bear in mind that prior to this, I had *no* clue what a concussion was and that it was actually something that involved your brain. Based on the minimal and passive information I had received my understanding was that this would be all over in a couple of days. So, Natalee and I went back to my mom's with hopes that Tylenol and some rest would remedy this whole ordeal. However, about a week later I noticed that I couldn't move my toes. In shock I told my mom and she said I needed to go to the hospital.

If you're old school you will remember the line in the song *Telephone to Glory* that says, "Central's never busy." To this day that's how I feel about my toes not receiving the signal to wiggle when I was trying to tell them to, because clearly my central was busy and the operator was on vacation. They were dead—I was staring at them hoping they would do *something*... Nope! I went to the hospital only to have a fruitless examination from the ER doctor who was trying to get a reflex from my foot, but again, nothing. He scheduled me for an MRI and CT scan for later dates. As the days went on my leg started dragging and I was losing sensation on that side of my leg and foot. I clearly recall being at physiotherapy and the doctor putting needles in my leg and attaching a pulsating device at the top of each needle. The objective was to get some movement from my foot and toes when the device would pulsate... *nada*! No movement, nothing! She immediately wrote a note and sent me *back* to the hospital and suggested I start walking with a cane. By this time, I had no clue what was going on, only that my toes were "dead" (so to speak), it was increasingly becoming more difficult to put pressure on my leg, eventually leading me to walk like a penguin—and now I had to walk with a cane. Being the woman I am, if I had to use a cane it had to be worth it, so what did I do? I bought one decked out with colorful butterflies.

I have two younger sisters who live in England, Candy and Jody, who would routinely check on me via calls and text messages to cheer me up. I would send videos of my motionless toes to Jody and report any updates. As she is a nurse and manager of her department, I could explain what was happening and she would give me pointers on what to do; in her strong British accent she would tell me the best ways to get out of bed to alleviate the dizziness, and send information that she found helpful. My family doctor eventually referred me to a neurologist but my appointment was three months away. However, when *that* appointment was approaching, I received a call advising me that my appointment was being rescheduled for another month.

By this time, my stress level was increasing rapidly because I wasn't getting any straight answers. I was responsible for completing legal documentation, application forms for short-term disability, not to mention now being engaged in an injury claim with my insurance company. Each visit to the unemployment office was embarrassing and overwhelming because I couldn't understand the process or documentation. The staff were very helpful and patient, often taking me to a quiet room to assist me. My regular checkups with my doctor became more and more discouraging as he would tell me that whatever cognitive and physical impairments, I sustained may very well be permanent; consequently, the likelihood of returning to work drifted from a time-frame of three weeks to three months, to indefinitely. I will never forget an appointment when my doctor gently said, "Where you're at is where you'll be at," after I'd explained the difficulties I had. You're probably wondering about the cognitive piece by now. Oh, hang in there friend, I'll get to that later.

My neurologist appointment finally came around (hooray for the healthcare system); he was a sweet, short Eastern European man who had so much compassion. It was a painful and lonely appointment that greeted me with long needles being jabbed into my body. I had to go to the appointment alone and had no one to lean on or share my thoughts or feelings with at the time. But I think the knowledge of a professional telling you all those red bottoms you have will have to sit in the basic brown boxes you got them in—for good—was the kicker.

"God bless you," he said with sympathy, after explaining there was no signal coming from the nerve responsible for the reflex in my foot, which explained my inability to ascend and descend stairs or even stand on my tippy toes. But thankfully there is a God (I just didn't remember about Him in that capacity yet). Insert yet another referral here… Off to the neurosurgeon we went, to discuss the possibility of surgery on my spine—a few months later, of course.

The following year I began to apply for support service assessments and assistance—most of these appointments were cancelled due to a lack of insurance coverage. By mid-spring, I began to paint to express myself, given that I couldn't write poetry as I had done prior to the accident. After painting one day I began to feel pressure in my head and I couldn't speak; the PSW called the ambulance while I lay on the sofa motionless and lost. The paramedic was asking me questions, to which I could only respond by his encouraged command of squeezing his thumb. I was terrified. Again, I ended up in the ER, only this time in a room with my family around me. I remember one doctor lifting my leg and it dropped like a log, he said he'd never seen anything like that—I still couldn't speak. I spent one month in the darn place only to be told they couldn't find any seizure activity in my brain and the CT and MRI scans showed nothing. Still, they sent me home (which I was very happy about) despite the fact that I had been in a horrific car accident, pretty much telling me that I needed psychological help. By now my medical charts might have been flagged, because I filed a number of complaints.

For the next few months of this grueling journey, I continued to experience all the negatives associated with the Ontario Health Care System. One doctor wrote a very lengthy report trying to support me, noting a clear neurological issue and frustratingly questioned why I kept being passed around. I often felt like most of the doctors looked at me like *the black girl trying to get insurance money*, simply cold and judgmental and lacking patience and compassion. They would be pleasant at the onset of an appointment, but once I would explain I had a motor vehicle accident their demeanor changed and the eagerness to help left, together with the once-evident attentive ears they'd had at the start of the appointment—one even rolled her eyes, tossed my medical report aside while stating "What is this? I don't know what this is," and began to text on her phone while telling my PSW Maria and my boyfriend Mark to stop helping me because she couldn't help me.

My occupational therapist, Kristin, was a saint. She dedicated so much time, research and effort into my injuries and was there with me at every appointment once she was hired. She asked me to complete daily charts, with ranks from 1 to 10 that would show when I got tired or over-stimulated, with a plethora of options, each having its own score. We noticed that the symptoms I had happened whenever I watched too much television, or spent too much time trying to read—pretty much whenever I was over-stimulated. Daily I completed the chart, and got the hang of what was a 10, and what wasn't on the scale. Kristin decorated my home with accessibility-friendly tools to help me get through my days as best as I could. She created a nifty little cut-out square to help me read: my job was to put it on top of whatever I was reading and it would highlight a few words while simultaneously blocking the other words out so I wouldn't get confused. When I explained that it was hard to look up, cross my eyes or focus when objects were close, she brought me a pair of glasses that had the same idea as horse blinders to help, as I had difficulty with eye convergence. Since my penmanship was lacking, she helped me get a nifty laptop to make things a bit easier for me. Kristen was God-sent! My insurance company refused most of my treatment plans and expenses, so she did her best to accommodate my budget. Thankfully, I had a healthy private insurance through my job which helped a bit. For me, every noise was intensified—be it a footstep, a closing door, a dripping pipe, everything. Just like my lip-gloss, I made sure to have a case of waxed earplugs in my purse all the time.

After a number of hearing tests I found myself in a quaint office with friendly staff members who specialized in hearing impairment. This would be my second appointment after an initial assessment and applications for a hearing aid. I sat in the waiting room with my driver, a pleasant older gentleman, who became my waiting room buddy for my appointments when

I was in between PSWs. We looked at the delectable spread of teas, coffee flavors and treats for patients; while I just sat quietly wondering what would become of this appointment since I had been bounced around from place to place for so long. The ringing in my ears was relentless, but as much as my ears were sensitive, it was at the same time harder for me to hear out of one ear. I would normally lean my head at an angle to hear properly, and like an old lady request clarification with "Huh? Say that again?" — it was so annoying. The possibility of a hearing aid came up in the discussion, but I doubted the likelihood of any assistance heading my way.

"Alexis." A tall, cheerful lady came around the corner, welcomed me and instructed me to follow her into her office. She was so pleasant and had a warm smile. Stephanie was a hearing specialist who had received my medical reports and looked quite happy to help. I remember that her office was laden with orchids across her office windowsill. She encouraged me to make myself comfortable after reviewing some information on her computer screen; as customary, I explained my situation and she actually listened. Stephanie said she had to perform a routine examination before getting to the meat of the matter—she seemed more excited than me. After a few moments she returned to the office with a whole kit and caboodle. I thought to myself, *no freakin way!* She came with a color selection of some sleek and discreet hearing aids. I couldn't believe it! After I'd selected my color, she showed me how to operate, clean and adjust it. Then the moment of truth—she turned it on. Friend, I will never forget the feeling when clarity came to my ear. Tears rolled down my face with gratitude—I could hear more clearly. Stephanie gave me the biggest hug and began to cry as well.

I can't explain what it's like to "hear properly" per se, but it's a memory that I've held on to for certain. Again, Stephanie left her office, this time coming back with a small teddy bear wearing a blue plastic hearing aid. She said my story had touched her and she wanted to give me something that they usually only give to small children with severe hearing difficulties. She packed me up with all her contact information for me to be able to reach out to her for support, along with other documents. The hearing aid was also programmed to provide white noise to drown out the ringing caused by the tinnitus. Although this was helpful it started to give me headaches down the road, but it was great while it lasted.

Eventually I started using a walker and had to rearrange the furniture in my home. I no longer ate at my vintage claw-footed dining table that I had dedicated so much time to locating and purchasing, because the barstools would increase the pain in my leg, and I'd had a nifty bench installed in my bathtub as I could no longer stand and take showers. Basic life skill routines were too much for me to undertake; one day my PSW Maria was helping to put my laundry away, and with her beautiful Hispanic accent asked, "Where do these go?" (I can't recall what they were exactly, but I remember this happening because it shocked me.) I stared at her, realizing I couldn't recall where things went in my own bedroom. It was *my* room! *My* dresser, *my* drawers, so how could I not know where things went? This became the norm for me—simply not remembering basic things that were often taken for granted. Sometimes I couldn't remember my way home from around the corner. My living space started to look like a great marketing tool for Post-It, with colorful reminders all around: *keys, lock the door,* and *turn off the stove!* Mind you, the poor notes were futile in their purpose, as there were a number of times I left the door unlocked *with* the keys hanging outside, and left pots burning until the smoke detector successfully did its job if I was alone. I'll say it again—it was a mess. I was a mess!

I think I realized something was wrong with my God-given capabilities in reading and writing when I couldn't write as fast as before. It was if my hand couldn't keep up with my brain, and my brain just couldn't keep up—with anything. I had beautiful penmanship before the accident and then it started looking like "*crab toe*," as Jamaicans would say, or like a three-year old's script. It generally took incredibly long to complete a form, sometimes hours. My disability application took days, *plus* I had two people helping me. At one point I couldn't remember how to spell my name, and I think that was the source of much of the depression which plagued me; I couldn't help myself in the area that I was most known for and what had taken me to the top of my career. Simple instructions would lead to tears and I would become angry as a result of the shame and frustration. How could a university graduate working in the court system not recognize the letter "D"? Reading out loud was a joke (I say that sarcastically). I recall a friend helping me to read the Bible on the phone and her husband chuckling in the background—yeah, embarrassing. It got to the point where I just didn't read any forms handed to me and I didn't even want to ask for help. When you lose the one thing you've prided yourself on, it's devastating.

To be truthful, I didn't know myself outside of school and work; therefore, when all that was gone—was taken—I felt like I had no purpose. I felt like a mere shell of my former self. Numbers were more than difficult for me. I didn't know I couldn't count money until the day Mark took me to Pier One for some shopping to try to cheer me up. A beautiful hand-beaded table runner caught my eye and I was excited that it was on sale. When the cashier told me the amount, excitedly I reached for the cash in my wallet and suddenly I froze… I burst into bitter tears right there in front of everyone during the holiday shopping season. I simply could not count the money! I did not know how much to give the lady, and I did not even know how much I would get as change. I just could not wrap my head around it. There I was, a grown woman in a store, unable to count money! To lessen the horror and soothe my panicking, Mark made a joke saying,

"She's so excited about the deal," and quickly paid for the table runner. I felt so embarrassed and ashamed—the professional shopper couldn't even shop on her own.

My bills were either late, overpaid or underpaid, and I didn't have the humility to ask for help. I wanted everyone to know that I was okay and could handle it—all of it—as I had always done. However, I was the only one who was in denial. No matter how much I saw my little canoe on that river of denial capsizing, I paddled with every ounce of gumption that I could, just to keep afloat, only to realize later that I was sinking. I didn't want help! I told myself that I didn't need anyone's help. Subsequently, I was very angry with myself if I ended up having to ask for it, let alone having to sit there and be spoken to like a five-year-old with every syllable enunciated as if it were an episode of Sesame Street. I had never been one to have a potty-mouth, but let me tell you how those colorful words decorated my vocabulary like a trucker. With Kristin's support I got some children's math books: grades three to five. I had to start at grade three and ended up video calling my sister Paula with tears in my eyes asking her to help me with two-digit subtraction. With patience and grace she would gently say: "It's okay, Lexy, keep going, you'll get it." I was unable to recall how to count with my fingers; I literally did not know where to begin.

As the months turned into years, my writing and processing slowed, and understanding complex statements and directives was just too much for me to handle. Mark and I made a hand signal that would indicate, "I don't understand," if we ever went out and engaged in casual conversations with others—I would scratch the palm of his hand. It would be at that point he would change the conversation or say we had to leave because of some made up story. I held his hand literally everywhere we went; the outside world grew more and more scary as my ability to function on my own slowly vanished. I relied on him for everything because I couldn't do anything on my own. I couldn't drive, walk up and down staircases, cook, and sometimes I had no independence in the restroom—he became my mouthpiece and my mobility. Our relationship was not doing well, because we argued often and I felt alone even though he was physically present. I remember at times telling him, "I understand if you want to leave me, because no one wants to be with someone like this."

He would say, "In sickness and health, Lex. I'm not leaving you."

Eventually, the long-anticipated appointment with a renowned neurosurgeon who worked with the city's professional athletes came around. Both Kristin and I were looking forward to it. We got to this swanky medical clinic with beautiful young staff members—I liked it there! Everyone was fashionable and upbeat.

In any event, after the consultation the neurosurgeon said I needed a particular brain scan called a SPECT, which was not well known in Ontario (go figure). He didn't hesitate to get me where I needed to be as soon as possible; the only thing about *as soon as possible* was that my appointment wouldn't take place until January 2019… the accident had been in 2017. When I told him about the business I had started prior to the accident he was so encouraging and kept advocating for me to return to it once I was fully recovered—he was part of the *hope puzzle*. My ability to manage highly stimulating environments was at a minimum; consequently, staying in dark quiet rooms became the norm. I hated it—the life of the party had become the loner, the outcast. I was alone, and I felt so lonely. Talking too much was too stimulating, listening too much was too stimulating, and everything was simply just too much. When I explained this during the appointment, the neurosurgeon validated everything—no smirks, no demeaning questions or comments—he understood everything.

It was at the end of winter in 2019 and I was sitting in the neurosurgeon's office nervously waiting for him to tell me what the SPECT scan had shown. Everyone was at the edge of their seat, waiting earnestly for the results. Friend, at this point I was exhausted and no one had believed I had issues related to head trauma because the MRI and CT scans had shown no bleeding in my brain or skull fracture; however, those tests had been taken months after the accident. I had been dismissed, smirked at and told I needed psychiatric care. At this point, I'd pretty much given up and wanted nothing more to do with tests, doctors, specialists—nothing. But today, here he was, coming into his office, not in his regular swanky attire, but just some workout clothes, and I remembered him telling me he would normally dress up when he knew I was coming for my appointments because of my involvement in fashion. We would routinely chat it up about great fashion houses and what stores or boutiques were the best options, but today was different and I couldn't really read his face. He was speaking and all I heard was, "I knew it… you have a traumatic brain injury…" I cried. I sat there and broke down weeping.

For two years these people had emotionally and mentally abused me about the difficulties that I was experiencing, difficulties that I could not explain because I simply had no words for what I felt. People who worked in healthcare, who were supposed to be compassionate and caring, had made me feel even more inferior for the injuries I was already burdened with, but just like that I felt a release. But now what? All this time had passed and I had not received any of the proper help for TBI-related issues. I had an occupational therapist who had done the best she could with the information she had, but now what? I kept thinking: *how can I fix this? Where do I go now? Who do I turn to now that this is the last appointment with the only specialist I feel comfortable with?* Because clearly, he knew *exactly* what was happening and didn't for a minute make me feel like crawling into a shell… what now? I just cried all the way home.

After the diagnosis, Kristin and I wasted no time in creating a detailed list reviewing my current activities and skill-building exercises. We looked at what was working and what could be changed based on the information we'd received at the neurosurgeon's office. We both agreed that I should purchase a workbook specifically designed to help people with TBI. In no time I'd laced up my bootstraps and dedicated time every day to the large print book that would later aid in improving some of the difficulties I had experienced.

My aim was to get back to the normal that I'd once had. At the beginning it would take days for me just to read the instructions for a test, and then I would have to read it over just to understand what was required of me. I struggled between disappointment and frustration, but I kept at it. For instance, a simple word search specifically created with symbols and numbers would take forever and left me with a headache each time. Thankfully, eventually each task became more manageable and seeing my progress gave me encouragement and boosted my self-confidence.

In addition, my neurosurgeon also put me on a new diet, which unfortunately meant I had to end my loving relationship with pastries and ice cream, or anything sugary for that matter. No white rice, no wine, no white pasta, no dumplings (in fact none of the good stuff). I was introduced to quinoa for the first time in my life, and quite frankly it was an introduction that took a while for me to appreciate. Moreover, considering the lack of in-depth knowledge around the complexities that walk hand in hand with a TBI, Kristin registered me for a conference hosted by the Ontario Brain Injury Association in the hope that my family and I would be strengthened with more tips and resources to heal and recover in the best way possible. It was daunting. Mark, my mother, and I had to plan a proper schedule for me, since the conference was a full day event. Waking up early in the mornings was challenging for me—which was a task in itself—not to mention the lengthy commute to the downtown core. It didn't take too much time during the event for me to end up in a designated quiet room for survivors while my mom and Mark attended the workshops, which produced a $60 meal plan for TBI survivors—Mark thought it was a good investment.

I was happy to know there were so many others who understood and had even experienced the grief I was living in, but at the same time I wanted to be present and participate with those who could manage all the presentations. At the end of the conference there were obvious stares across the room, and only those who had the courage would ask the one-million-dollar question: "So, what happened to you?" Although we all looked like war veterans, sporting various mobility devices ranging from walkers and canes to wheelchairs as some sort of badge of honor, it felt strangely comforting… and I didn't feel like I was the odd one out. We all understood the need for dimmed lights and quiet surroundings, and we all understood compassion and understanding in our own right—we were all aware of the injury no one could see. Seemingly we were all members of a secret society, which we definitely had not subscribed to, but ended up paying monthly membership fees for with our lives. I don't remember the drive home, but I do know that I felt a sense of relief, knowing there was a whole association dedicated to providing awareness, support and services for people like me.

"Oh, hey Alexis!"

That was Kristin's greeting whenever she spoke to me over the phone or in person. She had long, curly brown hair and a bright smile with perfectly straight teeth. One afternoon she emptied her backpack of new forms I hadn't seen before; she seemed really excited, which, in turn, was infectious—*what does she have now?* I wondered. It was exciting indeed: goals! The great part about it was everything was based on what I wanted, and it wasn't dictated by her; among the boxes to check off was my longing to spend time in Chapters, the local bookstore that had once been my getaway. Mark had attempted a pick-me-up trip there, but we quickly had to leave because the words on the spines of all the books were too overwhelming for me to process, not to mention the baristas brewing lattes and frappuccinos at the Starbucks on the other side of the store. Months later, Kristin and I started to meet at Chapters for short intervals in an effort to gradually reintroduce me to the setting; our visits didn't last long, but I was happy to try.

Significantly, and wanting to be a part of my journey, Maria would show up to work armed with great ideas and resources; in her kind voice she would say, with her heavy Dominican accent, "This is for you!"

One day it was a pack of Disney children's match cards to help me recover my concentration and memory; subsequently, we took turns every day flipping cards over trying to match the quirky Disney characters. We then graduated to putting puzzles together, from fifty to a hundred pieces. I also had specifically designed puzzles for children with developmental challenges; my assignment was to put them together each day and record the time each took. The outpouring of help was more than a blessing, and I did my best to utilize every morsel of it—and I hope you will too, sweet friend.

Surrounded, Yet Alone

If someone were to ask me to use one word to describe my experience in dealing with TBI, it would be "lonely." The thing about it is that people can't see the injury, so they always forget and tend to look at you as if to say, "What's wrong with you?" I've always said that it's easier for people who have a cast on or even stitches because that's when others are aware of one's limitations or sensitive areas, but when you have a brain injury it's like being a fish in a pond; you never know who will snag you. If you'd broken your leg people would know, "Oh yeah, you can't walk up the stairs." While on the other hand, when you have a brain injury you constantly have to remind people that talking too much is tiring and overwhelming—you're not just being rude.

Sound and light sensitivity were a huge struggle for me. I couldn't enjoy music anymore, because the lyrics and the sounds were too much to process. I even forgot the lyrics to most of my favorite songs. I couldn't keep up with the beats or rhythms, and totally lost my dancing skills (I still think my rhythm is a bit off… but oh, well). It became the norm for me to retreat to a spare room in someone's home because the talking and any background noises were enough to make my head literally feel like it was going to tear open or I was going to pass out. The mall? Forget about it. It was too much for me to process the customer traffic, the music from all the stores, bright lights, shoe heels clacking on the tiles, or even the sound of gum popping. The shopping queen could no longer set foot in her glory land! Most of the time I would sit in the car and wait for Mark or my mom while they ran my errands; I would watch people laughing while walking in and out of the doors wishing that that could be me again.

Naturally, the concern for my personal business venture saddened me. I had to turn down five contracts, including a photoshoot in Bayview Village, and an ER doctor who wanted to collaborate with me. The prospect of restarting it dwindled to zero; not only could I not count money, but I also had no energy or concentration to conduct consultations, liaise with boutiques, and I could hardly dress myself, much less someone else! My daily attire transitioned from classy chic to sweatpants and T-shirts. Before the trauma had transpired, you would never catch me in running shoes, because heels were my running shoes. I had to hand the grocery baton over to Mark because the aisles, with all the numbers and words, were too overwhelming for me to process; not to mention the non-stop beeping from the cashiers scanning during the whole trip. Now that you're reading this, you're probably just thinking about the white noise of the constant scanning that you normally don't recognize (or maybe you have and you feel the same way). If I were not at my house, I was in a room by myself in someone else's home. I started to feel like the party pooper because I always had to leave functions early. What had once been an easy late night for me turned into an impossible effort—my bedtime was 7:30pm. I missed a number of special events including (but not limited to) birthdays, New Years and even funerals.

The migraine pain felt like a burning spear shooting through my head and it was paralyzing and terrifying. It would happen anywhere and at any time. The trips to the ER became innumerable and unbearable. I am quite sure my visits kept their value high in the stock market, because every specialist would change my medication, which invariably would lead to some adverse reaction and they would simply allude to me imagining pain or just wasting their time. Every prescribed medication only increased the difficulty of my already obstructive impairments. However, the epitome of "trial and error" happened when one of the medications began to literally shut me down; I would wince in pain because I could feel something burning in my head. I recall Mark and my mom debating whether I should continue taking it. Carrying my weak, limp body back to the specialist, Mark laid me down on the examination table like a rag doll, while the physiatrist (specialist in physical medicine and rehabilitation) looked at the prescription bottle and noted the dosage was too high. He recommended blood work and suggested that I stop taking the prescription, which helped.

Emotional Isolation

Physical isolation wasn't the only type of isolation I experienced—emotional isolation crept in like a smooth criminal, because knowing that people didn't understand me made me curl up inside. What's more, my dwindled vocabulary shut me down because I was overly self-conscious of how I would sound. Word-finding and getting lost in a conversation were huge barriers for me. Speaking up for myself was no longer my strong suit, since the articulation was not quite right; it felt like I was speaking a foreign language, constantly having to ask, "Do you get what I'm saying?"

Also, at times my speech would slur or I had to text what I was trying to say. If you were a cowardly bully, it was prime season to pounce on me (and trust me, some made ample use of the opportunity, with no coupons). Eventually it became too much, and I totally shut down—the once-confident, outspoken, type A personality became a pansy, or maybe even a guppy. I avoided confrontation (if you knew me personally *that* would be unheard of) and became passive and distant. Not only had I lost my independence, but I had also lost my voice. My mom once said in a pitiful tone, "You're like a baby now, Lex."

As much as it offended me, I knew it to be true. I was a grown woman with the capabilities of a child. To me life felt like I was a minuscule dot placed haphazardly right in the middle of a blank piece of paper. Nothing made sense and everyone was telling me what to do or not do. I couldn't find my way on that blank piece of paper, and I started to give up. The frustration took over and I didn't know how to express myself properly. Of course this turned into aggression and anger; I felt like no one was taking me seriously when I said I didn't like something or wanted something done a particular way. I wanted to scream! I wanted to break things just to release the ever-growing anger present inside me. Boxing classes and Smash Rooms were often discussed with Kristin, but my efforts didn't bear any fruit, so I sat there day after day with my resentment, anger and frustration. For instance, when I was unable to walk and spent all day in bed, I heard one of the numerous PSWs in my kitchen scraping my stainless-steel pot with either a fork or a spoon after I'd clearly explained there were several other utensils to use. Naturally, I spoke with her about it and she caught an attitude and walked away. Imagine someone putting a plate with a pita wrap with tuna on top in front of you… but you're wondering what the water swishing around the plate is, and why the pita is mushy—she hadn't drained the water out of the tuna can before making the wrap. I had already noticed the annoyance on her face. Some of them would behave as if I were in *their* home and just did whatever they pleased. "I'm bored. I don't like just sitting around," was the cheeky comment one said to me.

There were some workers I missed when they left as a result of circumstances beyond their control, but there were others who if I never saw them again it would be way too soon. What bewildered me the most was the amount of effort someone would put into working in the healthcare system, yet that same person lacked compassion, empathy and mindfulness. You can imagine the added stress of constantly having to meet a new person to help you and reintroducing yourself over and over.

I am a burden. That was how I summed things up. I noticed how people's lives had to be rearranged based on my needs, be it transportation, helping me read, wiping my tears, bringing me food, helping me go to the restroom no matter the time of day, adjusting the volume of their entertainment, and on and on the list went. I would see the hidden annoyance (sometimes not so hidden) and I wanted no part in feeling like I was the cause of anyone's unhappiness. On one occasion while at a relative's home I had to use the restroom, but my walker was downstairs on the main floor while

I was upstairs. Dizzy and weak from medication I tried to call for help, but there was no response. Beside me was a red iron chair that I managed to use as a makeshift walker; while barely pushing it through the bedroom door I saw someone in the room across the hall get up and shut the door to the room they were in without offering to help me. To this day I have never forgotten the hurt, in seeing them look right at me and just turn away. I began to ask God why He even bothered to have me on this earth—I no longer had a purpose and I was certain that I wouldn't be missed if I were gone. I started to think about how everyone's life would be so much lighter without me as a deadweight. I started to tell Mark to just go because he had no quality of life with me. I stopped saying my prayers because I really believed and was convinced that God didn't like me and was punishing me for *something*. Mark would constantly say, "I know people who are horrible and God hasn't killed them, so I don't see why you think God would hate someone like *you*." Whenever I was sleepy, I would cry and beg God to not wake me up; when He did, I was angry. I once thought about a relative of mine who had attempted suicide, but her life was saved; I began to beat myself up for not having the balls to even try. I figured if God took my life, it would be easier for me to escape the pain, loneliness and suffering that I was drowning in. I began to find comfort in the lyrics of a song by a rapper who spoke about his life being better if he were gone, and since I thought I could relate I thought about the lyrics continuously while lying in the bed, hoping that this day would be my last. But friend, I thank God for mercy! I thank Him for the compassion that I didn't know about, because it's the very reason I am writing this and it is the reason *you are* reading this! If at any time you feel you don't matter, or it's the end of the road, think again. Push and fight. Don't let negativity win because you are of infinite value!

I think it is important that I say this: depression is real. It is as real as laughter, and as real as the salty liquid that falls from our eyes, called tears. Why do I say this? Sadly, in Caribbean communities these tragic and heavy burdens are widely looked down on, or even brushed aside and invalidated. No one speaks about it, and you dare not reach out for help because the response would likely be, "You have nothing to be sad about." There was one afternoon when my mom told me to "Stop acting like an idiot," after expressing my frustration and beginning to cry because of my aunt's relentless ridicule during her visit to Canada; the irony was that the grounds for her visit had been to help me. It was one of the longest two weeks, having to wait for Mark to return from a trip overseas. If it weren't her questioning why I hadn't returned to work, it would be her comparing me to my cousins who were working despite their health issues, not to mention a sneering comment that she wouldn't help me when my leg was too weak to walk on. The truth is this: if you're from the Caribbean, you are likely to feel even worse should you disclose or manifest in any way the internal battles you face when you somehow don't live up to the unrealistic expectations imposed on you, either directly or indirectly. Your job is to carry your pride, and don't rock the S.S. Happy Façade ship… even if it's already broken and sinking.

In addition, the uncontrollable tears that continued to baptize my face whenever I was at physical therapy appointments led to my referral for professional help.

His name was Sunil. He was soft spoken, tall with a thin build, and had a kind smile. His office was small and bright—no fancy furniture, just a desk, a laptop and beige-colored file folders with a box of tissues that was always at the edge of his desk. The chair I sat in was leather and very firm, with the convenience of an option to recline. Sunil was my therapist, who I would see every week in the afternoons.

At the beginning I was unsure why I was even seeing him. In my mind it made no sense for me to see a therapist—I had been in a car accident and lost everything, what more was there to talk about? While I cannot recall *every* session with Sunil, I will say that he helped me more than he could ever understand. Sunil wasn't forceful or judgmental; he didn't use typical therapy jargon—we spoke, just two adults who understood the pains of life trying to figure out what pieces of its jigsaw puzzle fit and what needed to go.

Sunil saw me as a human being, a woman who'd met disaster and needed a kind and helpful hand; I wasn't a *patient* or a number attached to a file folder. This made me respect him and open up to him because he didn't label me, and I saw the sincerity in his goal to get me past the ashes and rebuild my life. He stoked the embers in the ashes. In his spare time he would research resources I needed as long as it enhanced my recovery experience and quality of life. Sunil was a divine connection—a Cornelius meeting—I believe that wholeheartedly. Whenever I had a negative experience at a specialist appointment, he explained the nitty gritty details about procedural practices that I shouldn't take personally; I never left a conversation with him feeling less-than.

"Here, this is for you to try at home," was a norm from him: be it children's sing-alongs to help with memory, color-by-numbers for concentration, websites and apps for stress relief and meditation or resources to promote my painting. Sunil cared. When I was unable to attend the office, he called and chatted with me for as long as I could manage. "You need to put your art on display and sell it," he would suggest every time I brought a new painting to my appointment; and whenever I expressed being shy, he would remind me: "You need to get your confidence back and be more assertive, Alexis." As the months went by, I increasingly looked forward to my appointments. I was always excited to report a new accomplishment or an enlightening thought. However, all good things must come to an end, right? "I'm taking a job in Hamilton," was the closing statement in our session.

Sunil had bought a new home and taken a position that was more than an hour away from his current office. To say I was sad and felt a bit lost would be a true understatement. He assured me that I would be okay and encouraged me to keep away from negative people and to think highly of myself. A few months went by and I continued to use the tools and encouragement Sunil had handed to me, but then I got a phone call. "Hi Alexis! Sunil is willing to come back for some of his clients on Saturdays, would you still like to see him?"

Oh my days! I was so happy! I had my person I could completely vent to (without judgement) come back!

Now, I'm pretty sure you might be questioning why I didn't feel this happy talking to my family, friends or loved ones as much as I did with Sunil. The answer is this: I didn't feel like a burden to Sunil, and I didn't feel judged. It's very rare that you can open up to someone within the Caribbean community (especially the older generation) about the challenges you're facing—be it emotional, physical, or financial—without it turning into a one-up barrage of how their problems are bigger and more significant than yours. Moreover, your conversation in trust, would then become the new headline of the next long distance phone call to the islands or the distant relative lacking empathy; not to mention, how *your* devastation has become the backstory of their current stressors, which by the way have nothing to do with you.

The first Saturday after his return was a cold day. I'd had a horrifying appointment for my insurance claim prior, and I knew I could vent to Sunil. He had a kind smile on his face and offered me samosas and tea. We caught up on what had happened while he was gone; in tears I shared how stressful the appointment had been and that I had lost confidence in my legal team because it was becoming more apparent that their priority was not me, but money. I had begun to learn how lucrative my case would be and now everyone was just seeing me as a gravy train instead of a person with a life-changing injury. I was a lottery ticket for everyone. There was no shortage of direct and indirect remarks, ranging from debts needing to be paid, unpaid sick time taken for other purposes proposed to be submitted to my lawyers, and in turn, reimbursed to them. One person proudly informed me about research they'd conducted with their family concerning how much money my injury could likely pay out, but of course this would require me to present them with the details of my insurance policy in order for the unsolicited sleuth to complete said investigation (that I had not been unaware of).

It was overwhelming and stressful. It is far from my nature to focus on the possessions of others;

therefore, it was very hard for me to understand why others seemed to be sharpening their teeth for what they only saw as a jackpot. As usual, with compassion, Sunil was open and honest in sharing the nature of personal injury cases, as well as being cautious about others having knowledge of the amount of money I could potentially be entitled to in my settlement. I'll never forget him saying, "I don't like seeing you cry, Alexis. You're such a nice person and I don't like seeing you sad." No labels, just compassion. As part of the course he gave me some assessment forms every few months to gauge my progress and areas that needed to be worked on. "You're getting better!" he said after reviewing my numerous multiple-choice assessments. "You know the God, Alexis. Many people can't say that." Sunil's framework was not fear-based. Also, while he was strong on doing the work needed to improve and recover, he didn't scold me if I didn't. He didn't aim to please the masses, but called bull crap where necessary, and was more about the benefit to his clients than anything else. The goal was for me to blossom into the strong and confident woman I was before the accident—and even better. However, after only a few sessions reconnecting with Sunil he had to

leave for India for personal reasons.
   I owe him a painting.

Friendship Bracelet

I was never one to have many friends as a child, and that followed me into my adult years. I often kept my circle the size of a dot, but having said that, it should be noted that I don't use the term *friend* lightly. I love hard and have been told that I am loyal to a fault. Like most, you build friendships along life's journey and usually around a milestone; my long-term friendships were forged during my years at university, work and church. I enjoyed the company of my girlfriends just as much as I would enjoy interacting with my guy friends. It is certainly a different dynamic and I love having the best of both worlds. Guys don't really care much about the nuances of *"Oh my gosh, you didn't call me back,"* and there's a stress relief in knowing you won't be the topic of a group chat over something petty. They couldn't care less about who did what, and really just want to kick back and vibe.

My friendships with women are colorful and vibrant; we talk about women's issues, fashion… and men (of course). We shop and travel, and who could forget the tears shed together after a tragic breakup or a good chick flick. I love my friends. I love the laughter and support, the undeniable treasure each has contributed to my life. They have all been there for me in their own special way—for which I am eternally grateful. However, while this all sounds like lollipops, gumdrops, *kee-kees* and knee slaps, sadly I did witness another side to friendships that I would never have perceived prior to the accident: grief and gut punches.

"Lex, your phone is ringing. Can you talk?" Mark would usually ask me if I were able to carry a conversation whenever my phone rang: listening, thinking while listening, thinking of a reply while listening, *and* talking all at the same time was as daunting as algebra for a kindergartener.

Many people don't even know how much we take for granted. For instance, the ability to have a conversation is *not* as natural as smiling; especially, not when your brain has been injured and is taking years to heal. I don't think some of my friends understood the gravity of my declining health, and maybe that's because for the first little while after the accident I would call them and we'd chat for some time, or vice versa. Some may be thinking *why not just send a text, Alexis?* But it's just the same: processing. "You've been through enough. If you can't talk it's not the end of the world." That was Jessie, *the* most tender and compassionate soul you could ever have as a sister-friend.

Jessie is from Newfoundland and has the best accent ever. Her dimples and sense of humor make her unforgettable. We met when I worked at the courthouse and we developed a friendship after weathering one of the worst workplace soap operas one could ever fathom. As a senior member of the management team, Jessie was fair, professional and fun—I admired that about her. To be truthful, I don't remember her visits to the hospital (which she doesn't hang me on a cross for), but she took it upon herself to make sure I had an outing at least once per week when I was able to, even if it meant sitting in a park to get some fresh air.

"Oh, Alexie," she would sigh, and have this look of concern and love written all across her face. Then to lighten the mood and in her eminent chipper tone she would tell me something funny, or ask: "What do ya wanna do, chickie?" Fighting back the tears while her eyes grew red, she once said, "I really thought I was gonna lose my friend," —she meant that, and I felt it. Jess helped me with puzzles, rebuilding my relationship with Christ, and even helped me learn how to ride a bike again. We would find ourselves by rivers and streams in the summer like two kids in summer camp, lying under willow trees discovering ways to just appreciate life. If you tried to find a picture to describe compassion, you'd find my friend Jessie's dimpled face right there.

Remembering significant dates became my Achilles heel; needless to say, I did my best to send text messages of love and support. Brittany and I had met in post-secondary school while recognizing each other from various church conventions; we'd both had long natural hair, worn jean skirts down to our ankles and sung in church—she out of talent and skill, me, not so much. We would chat on the phone, sharing hilarious jokes, and our friendship continued to grow as we became young adults navigating our way through growing pains. When she moved half-way across the world to work as an English teacher, we kept in touch very often. Also, when I went to Europe the jet lag and time change made it so much easier for us to communicate because I was awake during the daytime in Asia. She would tell me how simple life was, not to mention all the money she'd saved from not having to keep up with the fast-paced life in North America. Brittany and I called each other sisters. Brittany would text my mom to follow up with me to find out how I was doing after the accident; I'm sure I tried to explain to her the issues I was having and that communication was very challenging at times—especially lengthy conversations.

I was so excited for her birthday while I was still recovering that I sent her a "Happy Birthday" text which was received with a dry correction that I had missed her very special day. Genuinely I felt sad about it, but it was beyond my imagination to expect the lengthy tongue-lashing that followed. It stood out to me as if the words came off my phone with the impact of a cannon ball—she said I wasn't a good friend to her. I felt the breath escape me as I tried to sit up on my own to understand where this was coming from. She was upset that I hadn't supported her when her loved one had passed away; however, I was unable to put the usual energy into her circumstances because

I simply couldn't. The worst news one can hear from a friend is the passing of a close family member—I had sent her some messages at the outset, to which she hadn't replied. I hadn't been offended because I knew people usually want space when they're grieving. I'd asked my mom to accompany me to the viewing since I'd been highly sensitive to light and sound at the time and was still passing out. We stayed probably for twenty minutes, but I made sure to do my best to support her.

I was crushed! Hurt! How could she not be mindful of the fact that I was trying to recover from a brain injury? The pain I felt could only lead me to reply with an apology in hopes that she would feel differently. Distraught, I brought it up in therapy, as much as my therapist encouraged me to let it go because I couldn't manage that level of stress while dealing with depression, it was hard to do since I knew within my heart that my intentions were pure. Well, it would seem that this wouldn't be the first scolding I would receive for forgetting a birthday or an anniversary. No matter how I pleaded with folks to be mindful of what I was experiencing it was as futile as pouring water in a basket.

I was losing friends left, right and center. It was

horrible; on top of the anxiety that was already having a heyday in my life, I became more anxious about forgetting someone else's birthday or any other significant day for that matter. It got to a point where I would begin to cry out of fear when my phone rang, because I didn't know what I was going to get whipped about because of my memory loss. One might be thinking *why she doesn't just write things down*; fair enough, but how effective is that when you don't remember to check your calendar even when it's tacked to your kitchen wall? *This* is the type of judgement that makes survivors of TBI want to crawl into a shell—the judgmental tones and expectations. Obviously, we'd do things if we could. It comes down to a balancing act of wanting to be treated as the person people loved and admired, while at the same time being mindful that *a lot* has changed about our capabilities and personality.

"Happy Birthday, Yvette!"

"Hello my darling! Thank-you, but you missed it by two days." Fear washed over me, the anxiety of what had happened with Brittany dropping bricks of thoughts that I was going to lose another friend over a genuine mistake. To my surprise I was comforted with the most humble and compassionate reply;

Yvette called me shortly after and asked these simple questions: "Are you my friend?" With a tearful reply I affirmed. She followed up with: "Do you love me?" Well, I would think that was obvious since we'd been friends since the early 2000s.

"My darling, I have more birthdays to come. You've been through a lot." Thinking back, I can't imagine how missing a birthday by a few days could cause such a riot and catastrophe. I had always admired Yvette for her poise and decorum. She had been my interviewer and the one half of the two managers who'd hired me at the woman's shelter. Yvette is a powerhouse, a woman who has the kindest heart, but is no pushover by any means. I've always admired her and sought her professional opinion on any move throughout my career. We've leaned on each other's shoulders and share a mutual respect that goes beyond words. Often, she would visit me for no more than half an hour, because she was adamant about giving me time to rest and not wanting to tire me out from lengthy conversations.

The point of all this is to highlight the importance of patience and compassion. Simple acts of sincere kindness actually help with recovery. How? Because it brings cheer to the heart and brings some sort of hope, hope for more kindness, hope for more smiles… just hope. There is a proverb in the Bible that says, "A cheerful heart is good medicine, but a crushed spirit dries up the bones." (Proverbs 17:22 NIV) I see the relevance of having positivity on the inside as well as the outside, because it has helped me a lot.

Maybe as a survivor you can't change your surroundings at this time, *but* I would encourage you to locate within yourself the will to celebrate finding cheer in something. If you're a loved one or a support person, you can make a huge difference in the recovery process by practicing mindfulness and fostering an environment that is positive and uplifting—full of encouragement and opportunities for laughter. Also, if you are unable to support in person, you can send messages full of kind words and tasteful jokes.

My friends Shelly and Christopher would graciously bless me with daily check-ins. Shelly would make the effort to bundle her little joy, alongside her gracious stature, and pop by with sweets and the biggest hugs ever; her cheerful tone and smile always made my day. She knew I grew tired easily, so she would always make her visits brief; besides, she had to attend to her baby. Healthy friendships and community are so important during recovery because they encourage social skills development and a sense of belonging. Simply knowing that there are people who are rooting for you and are consistent with encouragement and empowerment fortifies hope, and is a push to help you get out of a funk.

Ways to Help

- Maybe you can buy the TBI survivor in your life a coloring book.
- Get them molding clay to help with fine motor skills and concentration.
- You can even watch comedies, small bits at a time, to have a good laugh.
- Spend the time to ask your friend or loved one how you can help and be willing and genuine.
- I would also suggest researching how you can effectively offer support to see that special person blossom in the recovery process. Even though you might not be able to enjoy the same things as you did pre-tragedy, you can still enjoy something.
- Be kind and patient.

ALEXIS LEE

Surreal

I hope you have some popcorn… and maybe a tall glass of water too!

Here's how it started: when I first saw him, I was twelve years old on my way to the corner store to buy cigarettes and a lottery ticket for my uncle (I know, right?) And there he was, playing racing cars with a boy I knew from my school; there were no words exchanged because I knew nothing about boys at that age, only that they were mean and stupid, which was pretty typical in those days. Not only that, but I also knew that I was sent to the corner store for a specific reason—not to stop and talk to boys. Can you imagine taking the longest time to do what you were sent to do, and then your strict Caribbean elders ask: "*Weh yuh did deh?"* (Translation: where were you?) You then proudly reply, "Well, I saw this cute boy and I decided to go and say hello." I am telling you it wouldn't end well… at all! I remember his hair was in cornrows, parted down the middle and braided down the sides. All I know is he was cool and I was a sheltered girl in awe.

Now let's flash forward to my first week of high school, which was quite an adventure for me, because I hadn't seen so many people my age with my skin tone in one place other than Jamaica—it was a total shock! Crowds and crowds of teenagers, gathering together in the various halls, which seemed so massive to me because I was so tiny. I had no friends when I started high school, and quite frankly I didn't know whom to choose; I was nerdy and out of the loop in terms of current trends and hot topics. By this time BET had burst through the Canadian airwaves but I wasn't allowed to watch it because I'd be booted off the church choir—secular music was a huge no-no. As each day passed, I would see circles of friends form while all I had were my books and a starch-pressed crispy uniform. One day in English class a girl called Karen approached me, asking why I only wore my kilt to school and not the permitted grey or black pants;

I explained my reasons—we became friends from then on. What a relief! I'd finally made friends with someone my family would approve of. What is more, she lived along the route I took to get home, which was great because I wouldn't have to walk alone in the mornings or after school. She was an amazing friend to me. We had so much in common and grew even closer into our adult years. Karen had gone to a Public Elementary School with a bunch of boys I'd seen in the halls. She would tell me stories about them, and one in particular whom she didn't quite get along with. Then one day I saw him; the boy Karen didn't take too kindly to just so happened to be the boy crush I'd seen when I was twelve—it was Mark. He was tall and wore the latest fashion as far as winter attire went; but what would I say to him? "Hey! I'm the girl you didn't see when we were twelve and I think you're cute," or "Hey! Nice winter jacket." Nope! I made a U-turn and saved myself the embarrassment.

As time went on, I ended up being friends with the boys more than the girls in school because of my tomboyish ways. They were all kind and respectful to me. One in particular was the brother of my older cousin Jackee's best friend. He would always introduce me as his sister to the other kids in the school and finish it off by saying: "Don't mess with her!" Welp! Wouldn't you know that *he* was best friends with Mark.

Senior year came around and I found myself accepted by the cooler crowd. One particular dress down day I decided to bring my camera to take pictures; by this time I had a part-time job and could buy clothes that were *somewhat* acceptable as far as church standards went in secular social settings. I'd also gotten permission from my aunt and grandma to cut my uniform kilt to an inch above my knees, along with some other skirts that were originally down to my ankles—yep! In my mind I was progressing from nerd to cool (if you grew up in the church you will *totally* understand the excitement). So, there I was during my lunch period taking pictures with my friends who were all willing to jump in and say "Cheese!" I took the risk of asking Mark if he wanted to take a picture with me, to which he handed me a dry "No," and a smirk. However, once he saw his best friend and other people taking pictures with me, he changed his mind. Mark and I would soon begin to flirt with each other, but I didn't take it too seriously. The after-school routine was to hang out in the front corridor; some of the boys would freestyle, those who were funny would tell jokes while everyone else who was accepted just hung around until we got the boot from the teachers. If I wasn't scheduled for work, I was expected to be home no later than 4 pm—no excuses! This became harder and harder for me, because it was fun to hang out and joke around after school as opposed to going home to cook. Mark wasn't always there, but one day he and I found ourselves alone and face-to-face with no space for Jesus in between us. He wanted to kiss me, but I told him no because I'm sure he'd find himself with another girl fifteen minutes later. He was a teenage boy and I was warned about *"them"* right before I pranced into high school.

Most days after school, Karen's friend Frank from her elementary school would walk with us along the way. Frank and I also developed a friendship and he would come to my front porch so I could braid his hair for free. Politely, he would sit and listen to my family routinely ask him: "Frank, when are you coming to church?"

To which he would reply, "Soon." He was funny and always a gentleman towards me. Also, he was Mark's best friend. On another ordinary day after school, Frank, Karen and I headed off on our trek home only to see Mark tagging along. This was something he had never done before, so I was quite surprised. He walked beside me while Karen and Frank sped ahead and I'm sure they were whispering about us. Mark, being the free-spirited teenage boy that he was, would question why I was being so difficult with him. I'll never forget his cunning question in trying to get me to agree to frolic with him: "What's your favorite chocolate bar?" I told him it was Twix. How could anyone deny a caramel and cookie bar—times two? He then tried to convince me by saying, "Well how do you know you won't like something if you don't try it?" Ha! Clever little bugger, but I wasn't falling for it. I had never kissed a boy yet and I didn't want to, despite how cute he was. While we were walking, a family friend saw us while driving his red sports car, and offered me a ride home. I hopped in the car, told Mark bye—and he didn't speak to me again for the rest of the school year.

After I'd graduated university, I began working at a shelter for survivors of domestic abuse; it was a part-time job and I thoroughly enjoyed it! I had moved out on my own into a spacious apartment and would routinely take the bus, but one day in particular I chose to walk. Amidst the busy traffic that summer evening I heard a loud honking. Now, if you're like me, you ignore honking and continue walking. However, this sound got louder and louder—I halted the journey to my 4 pm to 12 am shift to turn and notice someone sitting in a truck… it was Mark. I was in shock; nonetheless, I walked over to him. He asked me where I was going and if I wanted a ride. It was a short and awkward trip. We did the catching-up thing and by the time we could carry the conversation further I had arrived at my destination. No exchange of phone numbers, just me rushing to start shift change to relieve my coworker from her post (years later I learned that he wanted to ask for my number but chose not to because he didn't think it would make sense as he was preparing to move away).

Soon after, I started my career in the court system as a bail officer, and again I was blessed to love those I worked with and what I did. The courthouse was always busy and I'm sure it looked like an ants' nest from a bird's eye view. My shared office was on the second floor and saw heavy traffic for Family Court, resources and other matters. One day, while zooming through the halls, I saw a familiar face; a family member of Mark's who was always endearing towards me and would affectionately greet me with, "Hey friend!" We had a brief talk amidst the loud and frequent announcements over the PA system and lawyers frantically running to make their appearances. I told him what my role was and he confidently suggested that I call Mark. He exclaimed along with the phone number, "You should call him!" Our conversation ended and I was left with the option to call… or not. I did make a futile attempt and thought nothing of it.

Invariably, like many folks, my life continued with wins and losses—some more memorable than others. In addition, to help with a move in my career and as I greatly desired to save some money, I transitioned from my apartment into my mom's basement, where my relationship with my younger siblings, Paul and Paula, grew exponentially. We hung out a lot, but religiously camping out in the living room to watch various TV series was our thing. It turned out that Paul knew quite a few people I'd gone to high school with—which is how I learned about the tragic passing and funeral of Mark's best friend Frank—whose hair I'd used to braid back in high school. It was devastating for many people to hear, and I thought about the pain Mark would be going through, because they'd been extremely close.

Paul and I went to the funeral together—as expected, it was packed. While at the gravesite I felt someone tap my shoulder, and when I turned around it was Mark with a little girl whom he introduced as his daughter. He asked if I would be attending the memorial barbeque that would ensue after the burial which Paul and I had intended to join, so I told him I would see him there. There were hundreds of people at the barbeque to celebrate Frank's life. I spent the hours with my brother and mutual friends, naturally catching up with folks I hadn't seen from high school and discussing the fragility of life. On his way home, Mark happened to drive past me, and we exchanged phone numbers and he encouraged me to call him to catch up. So, *this* is where we got to call each other, and our relationship grew from friends, to exchanging I-love-yous, to moving in together years later.

When the accident happened, Mark took charge of arranging physical therapy for me as well as an insurance replacement car, which sat in my mom's driveway because I was unable to drive. He initially attended medical appointments with me and had a grasp on how to navigate through the process, given that it was all new for me. I moved back to our apartment and had Personal Support Workers come for a few hours each day to help me while Mark was at work. As my health began to spiral downhill, he increasingly became my primary caregiver and I pretty much depended on him for everything. When my nerve was acting up, he would literally pick me up and carry me because I couldn't walk, and when I needed help going to the restroom he was there. My pride began to dwindle knowing that I was like a grown child asking, "Can you help me, please?" all throughout the day. *Normal* relationship problems changed from opinions about what was considered messy, to him constantly taking time off work to help me get to appointments, and subsequently, to me feeling like a burden.

I always felt bad for Mark because I knew my needs were hindering him from his social life. We couldn't attend functions because I would pass out if there was too much sound or light stimulation, and our once-common interests in loud cars and action movies became a solo deal. When an exciting action movie came out, he would have to watch it alone in the living room because I couldn't manage. I often tried to make sure he was happy, to which he would say: "I made a vow Lex, in sickness and in health. I'm not going anywhere." Of course, these words are great to hear, but I knew my physical capabilities had changed and I wasn't the intelligent, high-heel-wearing, outgoing woman he'd fallen in love with… I often thought to myself, *who would want someone like me now?* If I had the energy for a social gathering, we had to make sure there was a dark and quiet place that I could resort to; not only that, but we also had to make sure it was accessible because I had to depend on a walker. It was embarrassing for me, but Mark said he was proud to be beside me.

Eventually the pressure of traffic and personal injury court, coupled with my relationship issues and injuries, overwhelmed me. I had zero control over anything in my life, which was a complete turnaround from what I knew before the debilitating accident. I was angry and felt hopeless. Mark would hold my hand and say, "Pray, hun, you always used to pray," but by that time I was certain that God wanted nothing to do with me. He would try to cheer me up with a routine of orchids, cards or pastries when he came in from work. We began to talk about getting married more often as he continued to express his deep love for me and wanting to spend the rest of his life with me. Obviously, this brought a glimmer of hope for me, and I would always question if he were sure. Quite often I would visit my aunt and uncle, Sadie and Earl; they loved Mark and wanted us to settle down. Earl grew fond of him and would often have little chats about *the big day,* so Mark sat them both down and told them that we had started making plans to get married. They were so pleased and excited. He assured them that he'd spoken to his parents and was ready to move ahead. Despite the problems we had I truly believed the love we had for each other would overshadow the disagreements, and we could work on our problems because that's what couples do.

Then the unthinkable happened—I had a panic attack. It was the most terrifying thing I had ever experienced and I couldn't understand what was happening to me. I worked in criminal justice supervising offenders for a living, so what the heck was I having panic attacks at home for? It just kept happening that week and I couldn't control it, but I just felt like I needed a change of scenery. Maria, my PSW, was so calm and compassionate; she would hold me and rub my back, telling me that I'm going to be okay. I thought of the Bible verse, "Be anxious for nothing," (Philippians 4:6) so I decided to recite it over and over again. After one of the panic attacks I knew something was wrong and just wanted to be around my family, so I called my older cousin Jackee to tell her what was happening to me. Her response was: "I'll pray for you." I was thinking to myself, *you'll pray for me? Lady, I need help now!* Being that she had been married to a pastor for nearly twenty years, I figured I could find some kind of peace and direction in her home. She agreed to have me over, but the plans fell through. I tried my other older cousin Charlene, who is also a pastor's wife, and her response brought relief and a sense of hope. After praying with me she said, "Come." I called Mark and told him I needed to go away for a few days and needed his support. During the hours-long drive I held Mark's hand while he held the steering wheel with the other; I didn't want to be away from him and he was concerned, too. Mark looked sad and worried, and while holding my hand equally as tightly he sought affirmation that I would be taken care of while we were apart.

One of the large front double doors quickly opened up and I was greeted by my nieces and nephews (that's how I refer to them) —it was an overflow of love. Mark stuck around for a few hours then headed back to the city. Charlene is a stay-at-home mom who homeschools five of her seven children; with her Type A personality and regimented schedule she had managed to put together a spa basket of goodies and a learning curriculum to help with my counting, auditory processing and fine motor skills. I had always known her to be a tough cookie, and for the first time I saw her cry. One night I woke up to her standing over me, holding my hand and whispering a prayer. My stay with my cousin and her family was for but a few days and I was determined to go home rested. I started to pray again and really felt like *maybe God does want me around… and maybe He's not as harsh as I was taught.* I started to feel a different kind of hope, but I still felt a sense of sadness. When it was time for homeschool, I sat around the table with my nephews and nieces (all of whom are in elementary grades), ready to learn. Charlene wrote an equation on the board and asked me to solve it; there I was, a thirty-odd-year-old woman, with the eyes of little people looking to me for the answer to a basic math question and I couldn't answer it. I cried with shame and embarrassment. With compassion, Charlene excused me from class to wash my tears away and welcomed me to come back and try again. The children eagerly jumped in to help while not so quietly whispering, "What's wrong with Aunty Alexis, mom?"

Thankfully, my cousin took the time to work with me, to look deeper into other areas that could possibly need healing. We took a trip down to the lake one afternoon to have a chat; true to her form, Charlene was prepared with a clipboard stacked with papers and pens. We sat at a picnic table and she explained in her teacher voice that my job for the afternoon was to reflect on me. I looked at the sheets she handed over, attached to the very feminine clipboard, and realized by the questions that some serious soul searching was at hand. Now I don't mind talking about my feelings, but I've never been one to freely divulge much of what's really in my heart. And yet here I was, under a big shady tree ready to clutch my pearls for the sake of one question in particular: *now that you're not working, you've lost a lot of your skills, and you can't wear designer shoes or clothes, who is Alexis?* Listen! If I could have lost my breath any more it would have been at that moment. I had a moment of reckoning: who *was* I? I realized I had a misconception that my identity, significance and meaning were wrapped up in my life's achievements, because that's where I'd earned approval. It was where I felt I belonged and now I didn't have them anymore…

this really hit me, and hard. I also realized that I'd buried a lot of my childhood pain of not growing up with my birth parents into acquiring things and over-achieving. Not only did I have to heal from the trauma of the accident… I had some *me* healing to do.

The Sunday before it was time for me to return home, I watched my cousin's husband, Don, preach via online streaming because I couldn't attend church in person. Among other topics, he spoke about my situation and invited the congregation to pray for me. My heart was filled with gratitude and I just began to cry and cry while receiving whatever blessing God had for me. After the service ended, I happened to be at the top of the staircase preparing for the burdensome task of awkwardly maneuvering my way down with a foot that had no reflex to bend. Friend, I can't explain it, but I just remember feeling this push to try going down the stairs *normally;* I thought to myself *well I'll try, and if I fall someone will come help me.* Then, I did it: one by one, with an offbeat and wobbly motion, I went down the staircase on my own. I couldn't believe it! It had been over two years since anything like using a staircase without assistance had happened to me. I showed Charlene and she recorded it on my phone with my little niece screaming in a panic and rushing to my aid: "She's going down the stairs on her own, Mom!"

It was a sunny day when I packed my duffle bag, expecting Mark to pick me up, and to say that I was sad to leave my cousin's house was an understatement. I felt different and I can't explain it—I just felt different and knew that I wanted to learn about the compassionate Jesus that I'd heard others speak of—whom I hadn't recognized. However, what I *did* know was that I wanted Mark and I to get married in a small ceremony so I could continue this search for the "compassionate Jesus" without a guilty conscience over living a married life with someone I wasn't married to. I was more than certain that he would support me when I'd bring the discussion up, since we'd already been planning our wedding and gotten our parents' blessings.

After buckets of tears and long hugs I headed back to the city with my bag and an arsenal of resources to perfect my reading and writing, find joy and get closer to Jesus.

Mark was always aware of my discomfort with us living together without being married—it wasn't a topic that I was quiet about. I remember it being either a Thursday or Friday that he was in the bathroom next to our bedroom speaking to his cousin, a travel agent, confidently seeking help to plan a destination wedding for us. A few days after, I asked him to have a small ceremony with our parents and siblings in the interim. He snapped! The person who was so happy to talk about getting married was now yelling and telling me that I was pressuring him into marriage. It was like I was in the Twilight Zone. Consequently, I attempted to remind him that, "You were *just* talking to your cousin about booking a cruise for the wedding!" —to which he had several reasons why we couldn't get married now: from him wanting a big wedding to "You constantly change since the accident! I don't know who you are most of the time! I can't marry you like this!"

In total I had counted ten reasons why we could no longer get married over the next few weeks. I knew deep down inside that I needed to make this commitment to God, but I seriously thought this man who had been telling me he wanted to spend the rest of his life with me would support me. Since I still wanted an understanding as to why I was having panic attacks, we found ourselves in a small office speaking to a therapist, who also happened to be a couples' counsellor. My session turned into a debate about the current crisis Mark and I were facing, and whether or not I was ruining our relationship. To Mark's displeasure the therapist said she found no fault in my desire to be married and further added that there's nothing wrong with wanting to honor God. Needless to say, that would be the first and the last time Mark attended therapy with me, since he believed there was a bias given that the lady was a Christian. As time went on, we grew apart, we hardly spoke and affection dwindled to a loose hug. Mark kept telling me that if I didn't "Keep things how they'd always been," it wouldn't work for our relationship.

It was hard for my injured brain to grasp why this had become such a tumultuous and dramatic dust-up between us. Why couldn't we just do what we were already planning to do, since we were already living like a married couple? I even told him that I'd spoken to a pastor who was willing to marry us for free—but he refused. Some mornings I would wake up to a sinister look on his face; it was like he hated me and I couldn't understand why. For days on end I tried to explain that I just wanted to erase the burdening guilt I felt; I didn't say, "Hey, I'm following Jesus now. Deuces! It's been great!" I assured him that we would have the big fancy wedding he'd always spoken about, but just to help my journey I wanted something basic and small for now. On and on he went about how embarrassing that would be, and how his friends would laugh at him, and this one had said this and that one had said that. I felt beat down; this was not how I thought he would react. Mark began to spend nights at his brother's, often sending texts telling me that I was ruining the relationship and that "The wheels of this relationship are going to fall off." When we spoke in person he would shout, "How could you do this to me?" and tell me that I'd intentionally done this to him so that he would break up with me, and so in turn I could keep all the insurance money to myself. *What in the living heck is happening right now? My case is far from complete*! Was all I could think of. *Where was all this coming from*? My health was on the line, and frankly, I hated talking about money with my lawyers, or anyone for that matter, because there was no level of compensation that could give me back the life I'd had. My injury wasn't about money for me, and I'd made that plain and clear to everyone. I wanted nothing to do with the game of insurance thrones as far as I was concerned. The tension in our home grew so thick that I don't think a tornado could cut through it. Crying to my mom with confusion one day, I asked her to pick me up so I could spend the weekend with her.

After the weekend the drive back home consumed me with anxiety, thinking about the constant arguing and stress that I could barely manage, coupled with my recovery. My mom accompanied me inside—it was so quiet when I opened the door that I figured Mark must be at work, since he normally played music or watched TV. However, to my surprise when I went into the bedroom his things were gone. Gone. He'd left. Packed his things while I was away and left me… alone. With a faint voice I mustered the strength and whimpered for my mom; she came in the room and held me in her arms while I sat on the edge of the bed in shock, feeling weak and empty. "He left, Mom… he packed his things and left me." I can't remember if I went to my mom's that same night, but I do know this is where my resilience kicked in, with Paula as a huge influence.

The first few months after Mark's covert departure left me nothing short of going to sleep weeping and waking up just the same. Yet more Twilight Zone moments popped up when I would see him taking shots at me on social media platforms posting that he was distressed and stabbed in the back after being so supportive. *Stabbed in the back? How?* Ultimately, it turned into memes alluding to women not wanting to share money with a man, which led to more questions in my mind: *what the heck is he talking about?* I posted nothing, and still haven't—eventually I learned to do what was necessary to ignore it all. I was a mess: the shock, the hurt, the confusion, and sheer embarrassment were added baggage to my recovery journey that I did not need. My nerve would still send stabbing pain down my leg, the migraines got worse, and I only had Maria's help from 8 am to 2 pm. Maria was worried about me and on a couple of occasions I saw tears in her eyes watching me in physical and emotional pain. Maria would constantly tell me to go back to my mom's, but I was too ashamed. It is funny how we take on shame that doesn't belong to us. Shame that is not for us to carry. Every afternoon before leaving her shift she would ensure my walker was next to me, my dinner and snacks were sorted and the key to my front door was in our discussed secret location.

It was after dinner one night that I couldn't put weight

on my leg and had to use my walker as a wheelchair—while this was normal the difference was that I was alone. While trying to roll myself to the kitchen the wheels got stuck and my strength was weak at best. I sat there trapped between uneven tiles. Consequently, with no one to help me, in panic and frustration I called Paula on my phone and without an ounce of hesitation she rushed over with her husband and her swaddled-up toddlers. Both my sister and her husband Joe helped me get into bed and took care of the incomplete and poorly-attempted tasks.

Needless to say, I gave up *that* fight and headed over to my mom's the next day. God bless my family! No one said anything, but the looks on their faces shouted disappointment and distaste with how Mark had left; for years they'd welcomed him with open arms—Paula had even addressed him as "brother." The more I thought about him leaving, the more I cried; however, the more he tried to justify and convince me that "I didn't leave you, I moved out," the more he created a petri dish of hurt, anger and confusion. I woke up one morning on my late grandmother's bed consumed by the shattered heart that had taken residence and precedence in my life. Paula was there that morning to pick her girls up from their beloved sleepovers at Grandma's. She sat beside me on the edge of the bed, put my head on her chest and declared in the most confident tone: "Don't worry Lexy! Your glow-up is gonna be amazing!" Feeling like I'd let her down as her big sister made me feel even weaker. How did I come to *this*? I should be the one consoling!

I don't know how long my stay with my family lasted, but I knew I had to go home and fight. It was clear to me that the longer I stayed there, the more it would end up conditioning me to not try to figure my sandstorm of a life out on my own. I was scared. My mom didn't agree, but I kept telling her, "I have to try." This is where I think the seeds of my prayer life were planted. I begged God to help me—with everything. I had to learn how to depend on Him. I wanted to prove Him—it was a hard road, friend. I fought with fear and a developing faith—but I fought. If I woke up with ten ounces of fear or pain I fought back with double prayer and by working towards small goals, be they in homework, memory exercises or by repeating positive affirmations.

In time, I got sick of the bags under my eyes caused by a man who'd packed up and left like a tourist in a hotel before 11 am, and quite frankly those bags weren't Chanel or Hermes so they needed to go… *post haste*. Asking God questions became the new norm for me; I found myself questioning Him about His *can dos* and His *won't dos*, which led me to think about all His miracles in the Bible. As per usual, my nerve decided to take a long break and left me in bed for days. Invariably I mustered up the courage to ask my compassionate Jesus to help me like He did with the man beside the pool of Bethesda. "I can't lift this Sealy Posturepedic up like the man in the Bible," I said, "but I'm asking you to help me. Please." Weeks passed and with Maria's unwavering support, I went from wobbling to the bathroom with her by my side and graduated to walking around my neighborhood with a one-pound weight strapped to my ankle.

The glow-up was in full effect, friend.

Talitha Cumi

"And He took the damsel by the hand, and said unto her, talitha cumi; which is being interpreted, Damsel, I say unto thee, arise." (Mark 5:41 KJV)

I'm excited about this chapter because every word is filled with my hopes for your recovery process, dear friend. The reality of trauma and losing the life you once knew, the plans and even the relationships, just downright sucks! Let's be real: it hurts to the core and there isn't a single person who could ever grasp what it feels like to have to rebuild yourself all over again from the ground up—but this time, with limitations. Here's the thing; it's a process that you have to trust. *So what did you do, Alexis?* Welp! That's the whole point of this memoir. I want to tell you what helped me, and in turn you can hopefully try whatever you're able to do for yourself.

When Mark left it felt like something inside me broke—maybe it was more than my heart. The rejection and vaporized sense of worth left me in what felt like an abyss of loneliness and despair, but that propelled me to get out of the funk and get better. I had no idea how it would happen; I had no idea who would help me, but I remembered the woman I was before the accident. I took no prisoners (so to speak) and I got things done. I used this image and gave myself all the pep talks I could think of. Sticky notes with encouraging words emerged on my bathroom mirror and dresser. Words like "I am valued and loved," and "Ignore the negative."

In addition, I started a vision book, and in it I would add corresponding Bible verses and magazine cut-outs that my family and friends helped me to gather. I would play gospel songs to keep me company while I was alone at home, and with tears soaking the book I cut out every picture that looked like peace, love and success. Funnily enough, I came across a picture of a high heel that had a ladder and construction workers scurrying around to repair it—I made sure that clipping had its very own page. I pasted quotes and even added some glitter and pearls to the pages just to make it more my style. Maria would patiently sit beside me assisting whenever needed. Before going to bed, I would have a look at each page to keep those images in my mind and when I woke up, I did the same. Prayer became my new best friend. For the most part it consisted of bawling and weeping about my broken heart and shattered life, but I did it, and I believed that if God is as compassionate as I had heard then He would help me. He would see that I was alone and struggling. Therefore, every morning and night I tried to read the Bible and pray. I'll be honest; there were many instances when I felt frustrated, but I still pushed. Then I learned about the promises of God while watching online sermons with Maria! It was like an eye opener for me.

What are you talking about, Alexis?

God's Promises

- "He heals the brokenhearted and binds up their wounds." (Psalm 147:3 NIV)
- "And we know that all things work together for

good for those who love him, who have been called according to his purpose." (Romans 8:28 NIV)

• My favorite: "…and provide for those who grieve in Zion, to bestow on them a crown of beauty instead of ashes, the oil of joy instead of mourning, and a garment of praise instead of a spirit of despair…" (Isaiah 61:3 NIV)

I held on to these promises, and I still do. However, while you're reading this, I don't want you to think everything happened overnight, or that I was walking around chipper and smiling every day—nope! It was a tremendous struggle, a fight. I fought to get out of bed; I fought to keep positive thoughts; I fought to go to physiotherapy.

But here's the good news: I ended up enjoying the things I had the grace to fight for.

I started looking forward to working with my physical therapists and even requested additional days where I could go in without an appointment to use some of the equipment and socialize.

I thought about the aching news from my doctor that I couldn't wear heels again and wanted to challenge that, so I brought a pair of my red bottoms to one of my appointments and told my chiropractor, "This is my goal." I remember her face lighting up with excitement, she was so supportive. I honestly didn't know how well it would go, but I wanted to try. At every appointment she would make sure to focus on my goals and even consulted with other specialists in her networking circle for treatment options for my other injuries. We worked on better eye convergence, balance, form, gait… I even graduated to standing on a balance board! One of the hardest exercises for me was having to lie on a mat while on my back and lift my leg off the ground; it may seem easy reading about it, but it was hard—and for a while I couldn't. By this time muscle atrophy had made my one leg visibly smaller than the other; therefore, I had to commit to continuous workouts to help rectify this, which I was told would be no easy fix. At home Maria would help me put my heels on while I sat on the sofa; I wanted to get used to the feeling of being in my four inches again. Once in a while she would hold my hands while I walked a few steps in my home, wobbling like a toddler playing dress-up in her mother's heels. Subsequently, seeing my progress along with the support of the team at physiotherapy, activated hope in me. The only word I can think of to describe it would be that I felt *alive*. Yes, for the very first time in a really long time: *I felt alive.*

Suddenly, inspiration started to appear from everywhere. For instance, my massage therapist was also an inspiration for me. She once told me that the quite visible scar on her forehead was as a result of being ejected through the windshield of a car back in India—the same year as the accident. She said she was able to work and take care of her family, albeit with headaches that came and went from time to time.

Addressing concerns about my memory loss was a treacherous mountain to climb. Again, I don't remember how, but I was watching a football player talk about his recovery journey from multiple concussions that led to his impaired memory. His mom brought him to a beach he had frequented in his younger years which led to a cascade of memories—especially positive ones. Following this grand milestone moment he and his mom began to venture around to significant places to spark his memory. This ignited another fire inside me and I thought of going on a *Milestone Memory Journey*. I jotted down the milestones in my life and came up with questions to ask myself whenever I would visit each landmark. I chose both of my post-secondary school sites, the church I grew up in, and the airport, to name a few. Each landmark would remind me of what I had accomplished, where I was at in life at the time and how I felt being there again. I asked some friends and relatives to give me a ride and they were happy to help.

When I graduated from college and university, I didn't get to purchase any of the varsity sweaters—I made sure to oblige myself when I returned to each campus. To help me focus on the positives each day that I was alone I started to journal, but with a twist—only positive entries. It began with video entries and later graduated to written ones. Each entry focused on the minute positive details of the day: what I'd had for breakfast, if I'd had a good laugh, if I'd seen a beautiful sunset, and so on. This also helped with my writing. I was changing… growing… blossoming. The thing about a plant is that the roots grow in darkness, and sometimes it seems like the flower is taking forever to show its beautiful and unique colors, but that doesn't mean nothing is happening. The roots are growing and getting the required strength first.

I learned of a small prayer group at a church not too far from my home. It reminded me of my childhood with my grandmother: quiet, serious and filled with love. I was the youngest attendee amidst the comfort and support of no more than ten seasoned women in the faith—many of them seniors. It felt like home. Every time Maria and I left the assembly in the afternoons I felt much better than I had when I went in.

Unfortunately, the backlash and chastisement I had hurled my way for building my faith in Christ was unimaginable, but I had already lost so much just for His sake and really wanted to have a better relationship with God. Consequently, I continued to seek help from a greater power than myself. I can honestly say that that prayer group was a source of comfort for me. I began to pray more often, and as time went by, I started to find solace in knowing the compassionate Jesus I had heard about. Sometimes I would begin my prayers by saying "Compassionate Jesus," and while my relationship grew, I affectionately started calling Him *Abba—my* Father. And while I'm still navigating the walk, to follow Christ in the light of liberty, I sometimes find myself retreating back to the fear of His condemnation—which is so far from what He wants for His children. Maybe that's the beauty of grace; He will always show us compassion and forgiveness as long as we seek it. I've also learned to extend that compassion and forgiveness toward others. Sometimes it's difficult, but if we require it from God why shouldn't we give what we so freely have received? That's another part of my recovery that I had to confront—bitterness and unforgiveness. I had to forgive myself for all the crappy decisions I'd made in the past. I forgave the lawyer who asked me to stay behind at court the day of the accident because I felt my late departure for lunch had caused the wreck; finally, I forced myself to pray for the forgiveness I needed toward Mark, to clear my heart of bitterness. I left him before the Lord and always keep him in my prayers. Consequently, releasing myself and others from a bitter place in my heart felt like a boulder lifted off my shoulders; when memories come back, I do my best to roll the boulder away by pausing and declaring: "I release you and the negative thoughts. I forgive you," and then I carry on. The more peace I have in my heart, the more pleasant encounters I have with others—no-one needs a Negative Nelly bickering and bringing down the party.

"Hi Lex, would you be interested in doing a presentation at my work?"

My mom called me on a late afternoon in the fall wanting me to share my lived experience at her workplace with her colleagues and clients; she is a nearly-retired Developmental Service Worker for folks with disabilities—some with brain injuries as well. I thought it would be a great idea, especially giving staff an understanding of their interactions as caregivers, and ideally encouraging mindfulness. I was nervous, but willing to make a positive step in my recovery journey, so Maria helped me to put a small slideshow together outlining the salient points about my experience with a TBI. The preparation process was reminiscent of my days as a field liaison teaching students about the bail process in court—it was exciting. The big day came and I was nervous. I thought about my speech and wondered if I would be able to express myself clearly, not to mention that I had been out of this type of engagement for years. There I was, quietly shaking in a room with over twenty people looking at me. I looked for familiar faces to calm my nerves and began my presentation. It was well received, with expressions of gratitude in the form of hugs, smiles, cheers, a beautiful plant and a card. In recognition of National Brain Injury Awareness all the attendees received a green ribbon that I had prepared at home. My mom's supervisor invited me into his office for a chat, and with great encouragement he extended an invitation for me to share more presentations in the near future—I gladly accepted. Shortly after this great opportunity I was welcomed to volunteer a bit of my time color-coordinating nail polish at a local nail salon for one day each week. I cannot tell you how exciting this was for me, knowing that I would be rebuilding my social skills, learning a new environment and having a sense of independence again. I always looked forward to preparing my outfits the day before volunteer day, and I would even try putting on a little mascara. In a way it felt like I was learning to put myself together all over again. My wings were growing!

While you're reading this you probably think I have it all figured out now. Nope! Although my self-confidence is significantly better, I still have some work to do; in fact, writing this memoir makes me nervous, but my intention is to encourage someone, so I'm looking past fear and putting myself out there. In a perfect world the trauma and pain I faced would be entirely erased from my memory; sometimes that's my prayer point because some things still bring tears to my eyes. Needless to say, I am much farther along this recovery journey than what I could have ever imagined, and it has taken years. I make an effort to create and maintain healthy boundaries because it keeps peace in my life. "Seek peace and pursue it." (Psalm 34:14 NIV)

Wanna know something else? I got behind the wheel again! Bit by bit I did things to become comfortable with the goal of driving. First, I sat in the driver's seat while the ignition was off; while that may seem like no big deal to some, it's huge when it's the place you sat where you nearly lost your life. I then graduated to sitting in the front seat with the ignition on. (Woo! Fancy!) Months down the road my stepdad took me in his old green Hooptie, and said "Drive Lexy! Yeh man, gwan!" (Translation: Drive Lexy! Yeah man, go!) The car would make all kinds of noises, as if the community needed an announcement that I was behind the wheel again. The material from the roof would hang and flap, pushed by the incoming wind from the rolled down windows (no air conditioning of course), but I was happy and that car will always have a special place in my heart. We made an agreement that he would sit in the passenger seat once per week while I practiced driving—eventually, I ended up on the on-ramp to the highway… at a slower pace, of course. Sweet baby Savior, I was back at it! Grocery shopping on my own was the next goal to tackle. As I said in a previous chapter, grocery shopping was done by Mark and if I ever managed to attend, I had to use the electronic buggies.

Gradually I managed to use a shopping kart; however, I had to learn and practice this life skill on my own. I know I had a leather jacket on with some light blue jeans—I was nervous. Why? Because this was the day the training wheels were coming off—my mom was not going to help me make decisions on purchases and I would go through the aisles alone. Her job was to follow me at a distance as if we weren't there together. It was overwhelming and I started to cry; my mom came up beside me and encouraged me to go ahead. I don't know how long that grocery trip was, but I'll always remember it. I'll remember the proud look on my mom's face as she waited for me at the end of the cashier's line to help load the bags into the cart.

The new improvements gave me more hope—it was like more light was peeking through the clouds. I don't know what's next for me, and I'm actually saying that with a sense of peace. I've had some folks encouraging me to return to styling; in fact, one of my previous clients sent me a text saying: "I implore you to start styling again!" I would love to, but there's a lot of catching up to do. Social media has evolved so much since the accident and I hadn't been keeping up with the trends. Also, as much as I have to learn life all over again, I would have to do the same for the booming world of online marketing.

I used to be the type to have every detail of my life planned out to a T, but now I'm learning to let go and let Jesus take the wheel. To be honest, I think that's the most important recovery piece of my puzzle. Life is delicate and filled with opportunities, and while material things are good to have, I think the most important are fruits of kindness, compassion, honesty, and a relationship with God. I try to live each day with gratitude for all the gifts in my life because we tend to take so much for granted.

So, this is what I want you to know, friend—**someone wants you to win.** I want you to know that there's someone who knows what it's like to be misunderstood, spoken down to, lost, confused, depressed, and at what seems like the end. Maybe you've even lost various types of relationships as well. Even if that's the case, there's beauty in your ashes in some way, shape or form; it's there. Talk to someone if you're struggling with depression and anxiety and if you're a family member or friend, support your survivor with these concerns and don't bring shame to the table. Listen and be a shoulder—losing oneself is a heck of a lot to deal with. Ask yourself how you can be mindful, and what support you can offer to boost confidence and empower. Success looks very different for each one of us, but I do believe it can be achieved.

Dear friends, *you are* courageous and awesome. What's your goal? What does the next step in your recovery journey look like, and how can you get help with that? I want you to always remember to be kind to yourself; when you're tired, take breaks. Have a schedule for meals and sleep (trust me, it helps a lot). Don't beat yourself up if recovery is slow. I've also learned that lessons don't have to be these big illuminating billboard signs; sometimes they are small and powerful. I think every day is a good day for healing, and what I've learned is that healing is a process and not a sprint. Trust your process, my friend.

I love you, xo.

ALEXIS LEE

CPSIA information can be obtained
at www.ICGtesting.com
Printed in the USA
BVHW050847170522
637033BV00007BA/183